AVE MARIA

Flute 1

AVE MARIA

F. Schubert
(1797-1828)
Arranged by David Marlatt

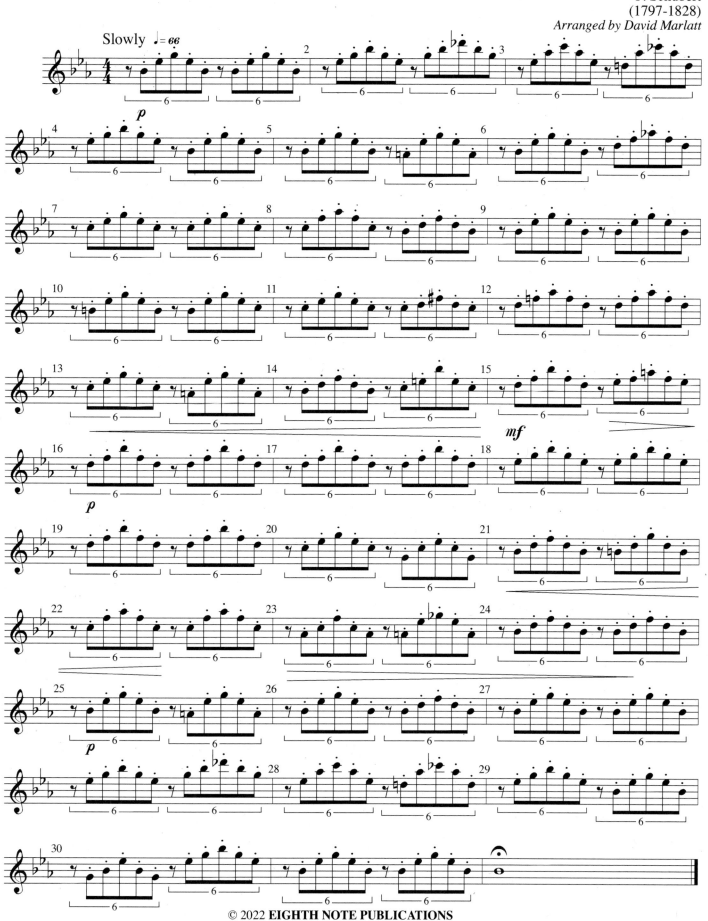

Flute 2

AVE MARIA

F. Schubert
(1797-1828)
Arranged by David Marlatt

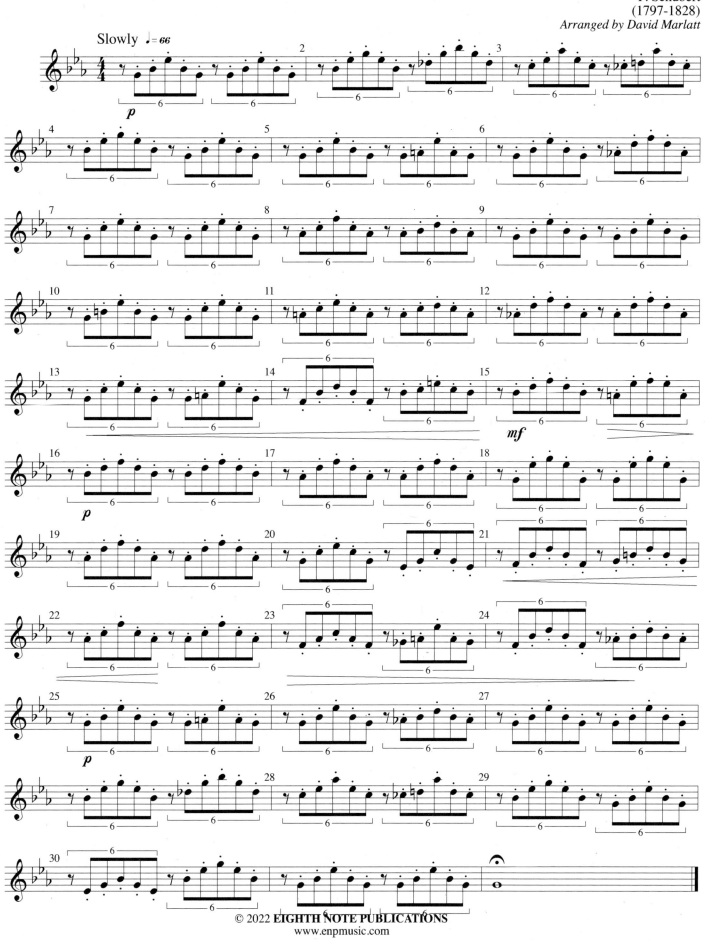

B♭ Clarinet 1

AVE MARIA

F. Schubert
(1797-1828)
Arranged by David Marlatt

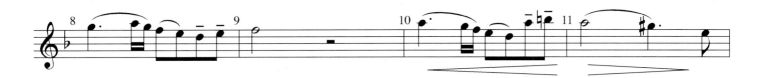

AVE MARIA

Bb Clarinet 2

F. Schubert
(1797-1828)
Arranged by David Marlatt